Foundation Stage and Key Stage One Weekly Spelling Lists

Introduction

'Foundation Stage and Key Stage 1 Weekly Spelling Lists' provides carefully organised lists of spellings to be learned by pupils each week. If this scheme is followed through Foundation Stage, Year 1 and Year 2, all phonic strands and high frequency spellings will have been learned in a systematic way, related to 'Letters and Sounds: Principles and Practice of High Quality Phonics Six-Phase Teaching Programme'.
N.B. Phase 1 consists only of speaking and listening activities, so no spellings are provided for this phase.

The spelling lists should be taught in class as part of literacy lessons (word level work). Words can be displayed using coloured felt tip marker pens in order to emphasise the various patterns. The lists may be photocopied for the children to (take home and) learn (at home) on a weekly basis.

There are supplementary lists for children who do not make enough progress and require reinforcement. For very able children, the second book in this series (Key Stage 2 Weekly Spelling Lists) could be used.

Following each section of lists, there are a number of 'High Frequency Word Reinforcement Books'. These books are designed to support the reading and spelling process through carefully graded lists of words.

Topical Resources publishes a range of Educational Materials for use in Primary Schools and Pre-School Nurseries and Playgroups.

For latest catalogue:
Visit: www.topical-resources.co.uk
Email: sales@topical-resources.co.uk
Tel: 01772 863158
Fax: 01772 866153

Topical Resources, P.O. Box 329, Broughton, Preston Lancashire. PR3 5LT

Designed by Paul Sealey Design Services, Wentworth Drive, Thornton, Lancashire.

Printed in the UK for 'Topical Resources' by T. Snape and Co. Ltd, Boltons Court, Preston, Lancashire.

First Published September 2006
Second Edition January 2009
ISBN Ten: 1-905509-19-7
ISBN Thirteen: 978-1-905509-19-5

Contents

How to Use This Book

N.B. Children are normally able to read more words than they can spell correctly. Therefore, most children will be working at least one phase lower in spelling than in reading.

Foundation Stage Children

1. When children have secured writing each of the initial sounds, and the teacher decides they are ready, the children may be introduced to the first list of words to be learned (page 8). These should be taught in the classroom and taken home to practise.

2. Children who progress quickly can be transferred onto harder lists at the teacher's discretion.

For Children in Y1 or Y2

1. These children should be given the diagnostic test on pages 4 and 5 at the beginning of each term to assess individual needs.

2. If children score 7 out of 12 or more on a particular 'Set' of words they can be assumed to have secured the sounds and word patterns adequately within that test.

3. Children should begin their weekly spelling work on the first set of words where their score is lower than 7 out of 12.

Examples of scores achieved by children on the diagnostic test:

	Phase 2	Phase 3a	Phase 3b	Phase 4	Phase 5	Phase 6
Child 1	10	9	4	3	3	2
Child 2	12	12	11	9	8	4
Child 3	12	12	12	11	12	10
Child 4	3	2	-	-	-	-

Child 1 should start on Phase 3b lists (found on page 26) because he/she has scored less than 7 for the 1st time.

Child 2 should begin on Phase 6 lists (page 52) because he/she has scored less than 7 for the 1st time.

Child 3 should move onto the Key Stage 2 Book because he/she has secured all spelling patterns covered in Phases 2-6.

Child 4 should either start on Phase 2 (page 14) or at the teacher's discretion may return to the Phase 2 Introductionary Lists (pages 8 to 13). It is not necessary to test this child on every set of words if he/she is struggling with the early phases.

Supplementary Spelling Lists

Following each main spelling list is an alternative supplementary spelling list. These lists are intended to be used by children who have already completed the main spelling list and are still not secure in the knowledge of the words at this level.

Letters and Sounds High Frequency Words Reinforcement Books

A number of Letters and Sounds High Frequency Words Reinforcement Books are found at the end of each section of this book. These sheets can be made into books (instructions found on page 3) and can be used either in class or at home in order to consolidate the reading and spelling of the High Frequency Words.

How to Make Read and Spell High Frequency Words Reinforcement Books

Photocopy the required book onto A4 paper. All folds and creases must be extremely accurate in order for the book to work. Creases should be carried out with a ruler. Always makes sure that you can see the 'Read and Spell' title page.

1

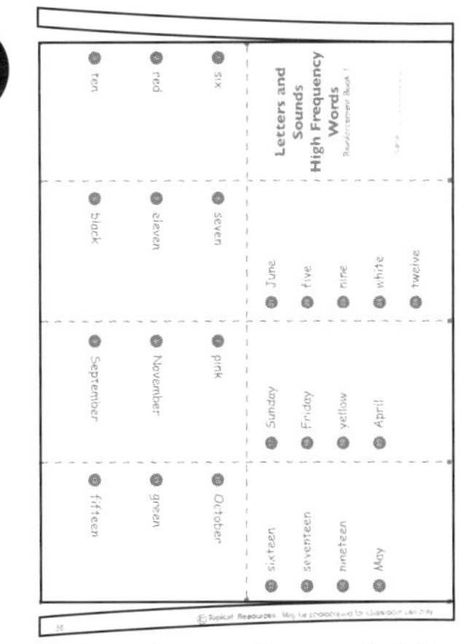

Trim along the solid lines at the top and bottom of the page.

2

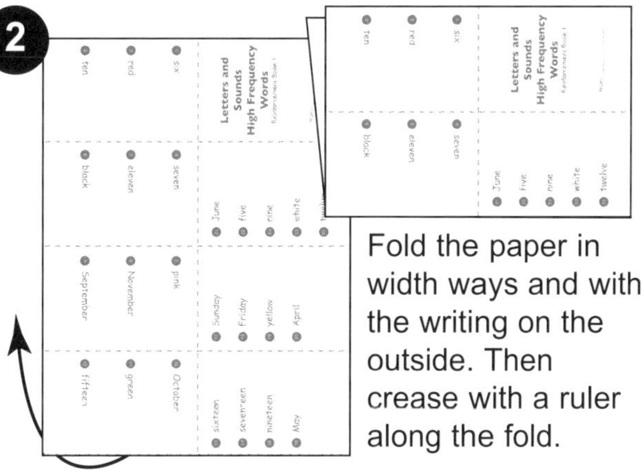

Fold the paper in width ways and with the writing on the outside. Then crease with a ruler along the fold.

3

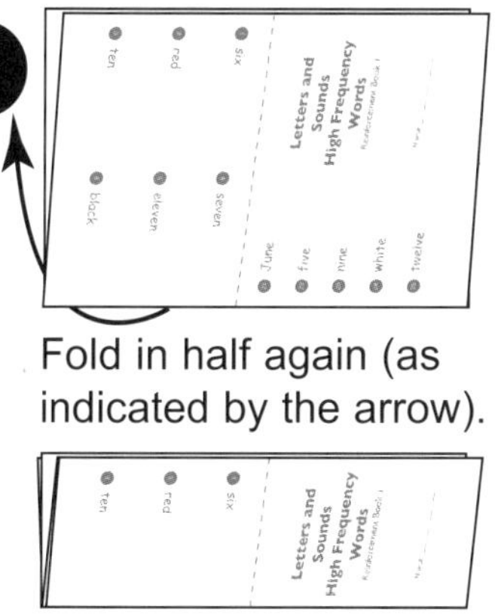

Fold in half again (as indicated by the arrow).

4

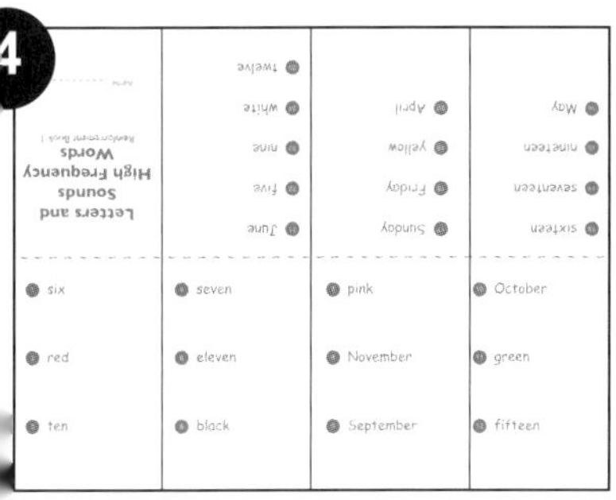

Open out the sheet of A4. You should have 3 creases making quarters.

5

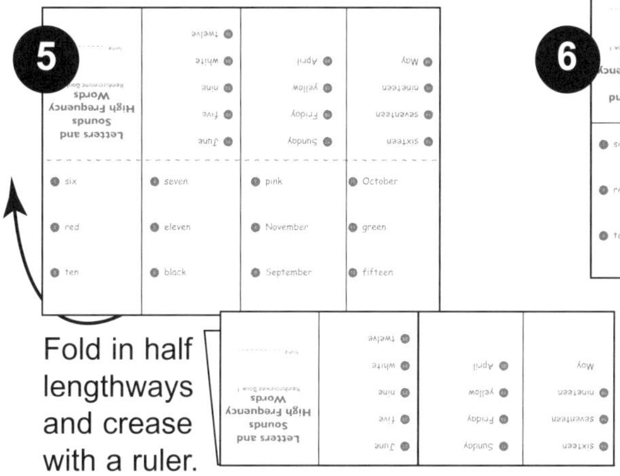

Fold in half lengthways and crease with a ruler.

6

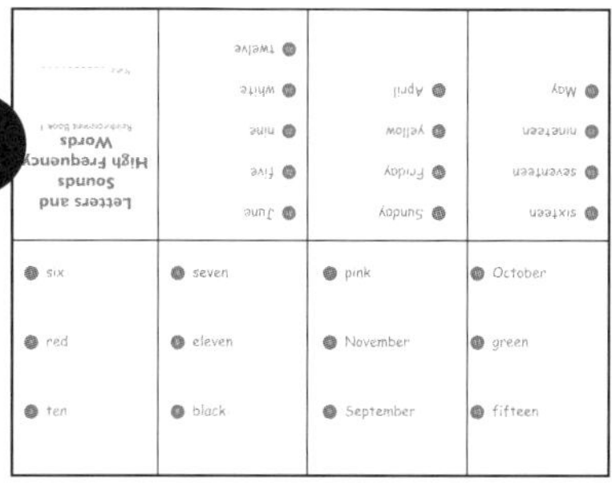

Open out. The sheet should now be divided into eight sections.

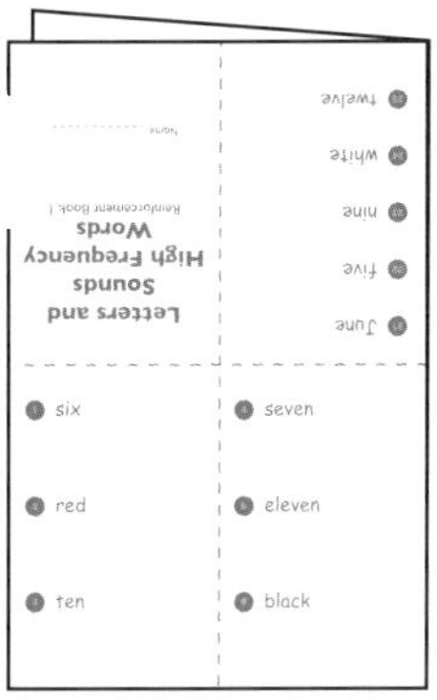

Fold in half width ways.

8

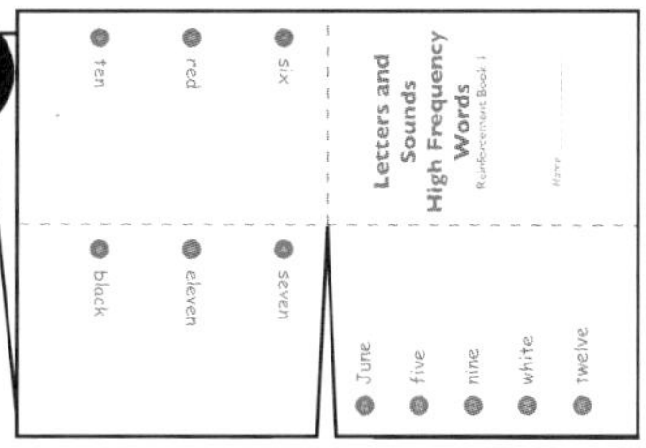

Cut from the fold through to the centre crease in exactly the middle.

9

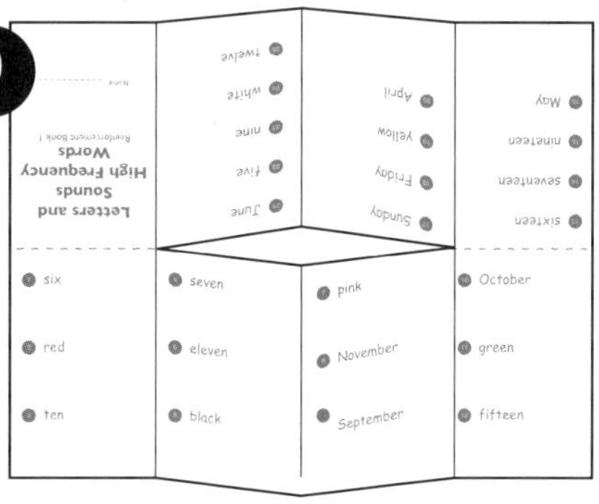

Open the page out.

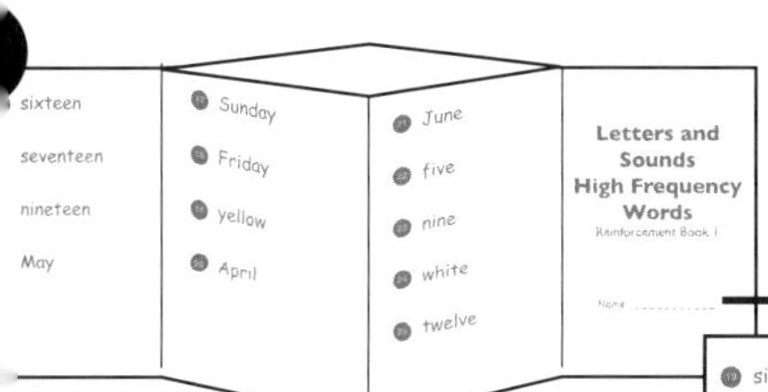

Fold lengthways

11

Push inwards from both ends until all folds meet to form four right angles.

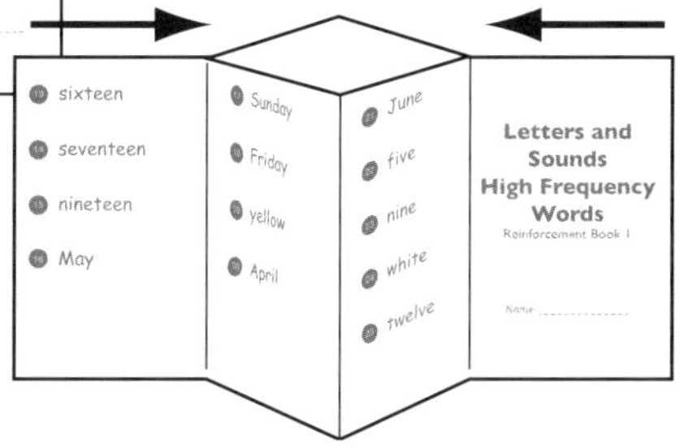

12

Close pages together – the title page needs to be on the outside. You should now have an A6 'Reinforcement Book'!

Diagnostic Spelling Test

Each word below should be read out aloud by the teacher, then put into a sentence and then re-read. After listening to this, the children should then individually write down the spelling in the appropriate space on their answer sheet.

e.g. Number 1, **cat** – The **cat** was sitting by the fire – Number 1, **cat**

For Reception and Year 1 children, it would be advisable to enlarge their answer sheet sheet to A3 size and then fold in half.

Phase 2	Phase 3(a)	Phase 3(b)
1. pat	1. jam	1. burn
2. sit	2. vet	2. boil
3. man	3. will	3. night
4. cap	4. mix	4. down
5. pick	5. yes	5. near
6. ten	6. zip	6. boxer
7. rug	7. jazz	7. keep
8. hit	8. quiz	8. soon
9. fun	9. chop	9. card
10. puff	10. ship	10. for
11. tell	11. this	11. sail
12. miss	12. sing	12. coat

Phase 4	Phase 5	Phase 6
1. fish	1. found	1. bunches
2. chin	2. cried	2. rooms
3. milk	3. shirt	3. liking
4. melt	4. amaze	4. worried
5. jump	5. donkey	5. skipped
6. bank	6. pitch	6. hopeful
7. spend	7. clown	7. flying
8. plant	8. seat	8. sending
9. whisk	9. further	9. tries
10. chest	10. cheese	10. putting
11. bench	11. nice	11. sadly
12. clasp	12. world	12. liked

Diagnostic Spelling Test

Pupil Sheet

Name: ______________________

Date: ______________________

Phase 2	Phase 3(a)	Phase 3(b)
1.	1.	1.
2.	2.	2.
3.	3.	3.
4.	4.	4.
5.	5.	5.
6.	6.	6.
7.	7.	7.
8.	8.	8.
9.	9.	9.
10.	10.	10.
11.	11.	11.
12.	12.	12.

Phase 4	Phase 5	Phase 6
1.	1.	1.
2.	2.	2.
3.	3.	3.
[illegible]	4.	4.
[illegible]	5.	5.
[illegible]	6.	6.
[illegible]	7.	7.
[illegible]	8.	8.
[illegible]	9.	9.
[illegible]	10.	10.
[illegible]	11.	11.
[illegible]	12.	12.

'Letters and Sounds'

Phase 2

Phase 2 Introductory Spelling List 1

Source: Letters and Sounds - in teaching order
Introducing: **s, a, t, p, i, n, m, d.**

Week 1
Date:
Name:
1 at
2 sat
3 pat

Week 2
Date:
Name:
1 it
2 sit
3 pit

Week 3
Date:
Name:
1 tip
2 sip
3 pip

Week 4
Date:
Name:
1 an
2 pan
3 tan

Week 5
Date:
Name:
1 man
2 mat
3 map

Week 6
Date:
Name:
1 dad
2 sad
3 did

Phase 2 Introductory Spelling List 1

Source: Letters and Sounds - in teaching order
Introducing: **g, o, c, k, ck, e.**

Date:
Name:

1. pig
2. dig
3. tig

Date:
Name:

1. got
2. not
3. pot

Date:
Name:

1. can
2. cat
3. cap

Week 10

Date:
Name:

1. kid
2. kit
3. Ken

Week 11

Date:
Name:

1. pick
2. sick
3. kick

Week 12

Date:
Name:

1. ten
2. pen
3. men

Phase 2 Introductory Spelling List 2

Source: Letters and Sounds - in teaching order
Introducing: **u, r, h, b, f, ff.**

Week 1

Date:
Name:

1 tug
2 rug
3 dug

Week 2

Date:
Name:

1 rat
2 mat
3 hat

Week 3

Date:
Name:

1 hit
2 pit
3 kit

Week 4

Date:
Name:

1 mug
2 hug
3 bug

Week 5

Date:
Name:

1 fun
2 sun
3 bun

Week 6

Date:
Name:

1 puff
2 huff
3 cuff

Phase 2 Introductory Spelling List 2

Source: Letters and Sounds - in teaching order
Introducing: **l, ll, ss (weeks 7-9)**
Mixed words (weeks 10-11)

Date:
Name:
1 fog
2 log
3 dog

Date:
Name:
1 tell
2 sell
3 fell

Date:
Name:
1 miss
2 kiss
3 hiss

Week 10

Date:
Name:
1 sat
2 sit
3 tip

Week 11

Date:
Name:
1 pan
2 mat
3 did

Week 12

Date:
Name:
1 kit
2 cat
3 pen

Phase 2 Introductory Spelling List 3

Source: Letters and Sounds (Mixed Lists)

Week 1

Date:

Name:

1. cat
2. mat
3. sat
4. fat
5. pat

Week 2

Date:

Name:

1. bet
2. wet
3. met
4. ten
5. pen

Week 3

Date:

Name:

1. tin
2. bin
3. pin
4. lip
5. tip

Week 4

Date:

Name:

1. dog
2. fog
3. log
4. got
5. [illegible]

Week 5

Date:

Name:

1. mug
2. rug
3. bug
4. sun
5. fun

Week 6

Date:

Name:

1. can
2. dad
3. had
4. get
5. up

Phase 2 Introductory Spelling List 3

Source: Letters and Sounds (Mixed Lists)
** tricky words*
NB. Week 11 includes alternative sounds

Week 10

Date:
Name:

1. big
2. him
3. not
4. got
5. mum

Date:
Name:

1. and
2. back
3. up
4. of
5. off

Week 11

Date:
Name:

1. a
2. an
3. at
4. on
5. up

Date:
Name:

1. I*
2. on
3. his
4. is
5. as

Week 12

Date:
Name:

1. if
2. in
3. it
4. but
5. put

Date:
Name:

1. the*
2. no*
3. go*
4. to*
5. into*

Phase 2 Spelling List

Source: Words 1 - 6 taken from Letters and Sounds Phase 2 Phonics
Words 7 - 10 taken from Letters and Sounds Phase 2 High Frequency Word List

	Week 1	Week 2	Week 3	Week 4	Week 5	Week 6
	Date:	Date:	Date:	Date:	Date:	Date:
	Name:	Name:	Name:	Name:	Name:	Name:
1	cat	met	pin	pot	sun	tan
2	hat	get	bin	hot	fun	ran
3	bat	pet	tin	cot	run	man
4	mat	let	fin	not	rug	pan
5	fat	set	pig	dot	mug	rat
6	sat	bet	dig	got	bug	pat
7	**dad**	**big**	**mum**	**an**	**it**	**and**
8	**can**	**him**	**but**	**at**	**on**	**is**
9	**had**	**not**	**put**	**if**	**up**	**as**
10	**his**	**got**	**a**	**in**	**back**	**get**

Phase 2 Spelling List

Source: Words 1 - 6 taken from Letters and Sounds Phase 2 Phonics
Words 7 - 10 taken from Letters and Sounds Phase 2 High Frequency Word List

Date:	Date:	Date:	Date:	Date:	Date:
Name:	Name:	Name:	Name:	Name:	Name:
1 men	1 hit	1 fog	1 put	1 puff	1 cuff
2 pen	2 bit	2 log	2 cut	2 huff	2 fill
3 hen	3 sit	3 hop	3 nut	3 bell	3 doll
4 Ben	4 lit	4 pop	4 bun	4 tell	4 dull
5 Ken	5 pit	5 mop	5 fun	5 less	5 miss
6 ten	6 hid	6 top	6 bug	6 mess	6 boss
7 **off**	7 **go**	7 **can**	7 **dad**	7 **had**	7 **get**
8 **of**	8 **no**	8 **mum**	8 **but**	8 **put**	8 **a**
9 **I**	9 **to**	9 **it**	9 **on**	9 **up**	9 **back**
10 **the**	10 **into**	10 **off**	10 **of**	10 **I**	10 **the**

Phase 2 Supplementary Spelling List

N.B. Only to be used with children who are repeating aspects of this phase's work.

Source: Words 1 - 8 taken from Letters and Sounds Phase 2 Phonics
Words 9 - 10 taken from Letters and Sounds Phase 2 High Frequency Word List

	Week 1	Week 2	Week 3	Week 4	Week 5	Week 6
	Date:	Date:	Date:	Date:	Date:	Date:
	Name:	Name:	Name:	Name:	Name:	Name:
1	map	pit	men	sum	dig	mat
2	tap	kit	pen	mum	big	sat
3	cap	hit	ten	tum	fig	hat
4	gap	lit	Ben	hum	pig	bat
5	net	pot	rug	hop	fog	met
6	bet	cot	hug	pop	dog	pet
7	pet	hot	mug	mop	log	let
8	get	lot	bug	top	hog	set
9	**big**	**and**	**him**	**is**	**not**	**as**
10	**an**	**go**	**at**	**no**	**if**	**to**

Phase 2 Supplementary Spelling List

N.B. Only to be used with children who are repeating aspects of this phase's work.

Source: Words 1 - 8 taken from Letters and Sounds Phase 2 Phonics
Words 9 - 10 taken from Letters and Sounds Phase 2 High Frequency Word List

Date:
Name:

1. puff
2. huff
3. cuff
4. doll
5. dull
6. full
7. boss
8. less
9. **but**
10. **dad**

Date:
Name:

1. tell
2. sell
3. fell
4. bell
5. kiss
6. miss
7. pass
8. mass
9. **of**
10. **on**

Date:
Name:

1. pan
2. lot
3. met
4. log
5. sum
6. pen
7. set
8. tap
9. **mum**
10. **can**

Date:
Name:

1. gap
2. lit
3. ten
4. rug
5. wig
6. hat
7. hot
8. top
9. **off**
10. **it**

Date:
Name:

1. set
2. sit
3. sat
4. sad
5. Sam
6. sip
7. hit
8. sun
9. **his**
10. **into**

Date:
Name:

1. map
2. mat
3. man
4. nap
5. nan
6. net
7. not
8. nut
9. **got**
10. **in**

‘Letters and Sounds’

Read and Spell High Frequency Words

Reinforcement Book 1

Name: ____________

1 can

2 dad

3 had

4 get

5 big

6 him

7 not

8 got

9 mum

10 but

11 put

12 a

13 an

14 at

15 if

16 in

17 it

18 on

19 up

‘Letters and Sounds’

Read and Spell High Frequency Words

Reinforcement Book 2

Name: ______________

1 *back*

2 *and*

3 *is*

4 *as*

5 *his*

6 *off*

7 *of*

8 *I*

9 *the*

10 *go*

11 *no*

12 *to*

13 *into*

Letters and Sounds Phase 2 Individual Pupil Record

Name: ______________________________

Date Begun: ___________________________

We can assume a letter or word has been learned when it has been either tested or used correctly at least 3 times.

Phase 2 Letter Progression

	Tick or Date		
s			
a			
t			
p			
i			
n			
m			
d			
g			
o			
c			
k			
ck			
e			
u			
r			
h			
b			
f,ff			
l,ll			
ss			

Phase 2 Example cvc words

	Tick or Date		
s,a,t, (sat)			
p,i,n, (pin)			
m (man)			
d,g,o, (dog)			
c (cat)			
k (kit)			
ck (sock)			
e (pet)			
u (mum)			
r (ran)			
h (hat)			
b (bin)			
f (fun)			
ff (off)			
ll (doll)			
ss (miss)			

Phase 2 Example vc words

	Tick or Date		
s,a (as)			
i,p,i (it)			
n (in)			
m (am)			
d,g,o (on)			
c,k,ck,e,u (up)			
r,h,f (if)			
ff,l,ll (off, ill, all)			

Phase 2 High Frequency Words

	Tick or Date		
1. can			
2. dad			
3. had			
4. get			
5. big			
6. him			
7. not			
8. got			
9. mum			
10. but			
11. put			
12. a			
13. an			
14. at			
15. if			
16. in			
17. it			
18. on			
19. up			
20. back			
21. and			
22. is			
23. as			
24. his			
25. off			
26. of			
27. I			
28. the			
29. go			
30. no			
31. to			
32. into			

Bold indicates "Tricky" High Frequency Words

‘Letters and Sounds’

Phase 3

Phase 3(a) Spelling List

Source: Words 1 - 7 taken from Letters and Sounds Phase 3 Phonics
Introducing: **j, v, w, x, y, z, zz, qu, ch, sh, th/th, ng.**
Words 8 - 10 taken from Letters and Sounds Phase 3 High Frequency Word List

Week 1	Week 2	Week 3	Week 4	Week 5	Week 6
Date:	Date:	Date:	Date:	Date:	Date:
Name:	Name:	Name:	Name:	Name:	Name:
1 jam	1 wag	1 box	1 buzz	1 chip	1 ship
2 jet	2 wig	2 fox	2 jazz	2 chop	2 shin
3 jog	3 web	3 yes	3 fizz	3 chat	3 shop
4 Jack	4 wax	4 yet	4 quiz	4 chap	4 shut
5 van	5 mix	5 yell	5 quit	5 chin	5 cash
6 vet	6 fix	6 zip	6 quick	6 much	6 bash
7 win	7 six	7 zap	7 quack	7 such	7 mash
8 **will**	8 **then**	8 **now**	8 **see**	8 **he**	8 **be**
9 **that**	9 **them**	9 **down**	9 **look**	9 **we**	9 **she**
10 **this**	10 **with**	10 **for**	10 **too**	10 **me**	10 **was**

Phase 3(a) Spelling List

Source: Words 1 - 7 taken from Letters and Sounds Phase 3 Phonics
Introducing: **j, v, w, x, y, z, zz, qu, ch, sh, th/th, ng.**
Words 8 - 10 taken from Letters and Sounds Phase 3 High Frequency Word List

Date: / Name:	1	2	3	4	5	6	7	8	9	10
Date: Name:	yet	wax	cash	chin	quit	yell	mix	**them**	**he**	**all**
Date: Name:	fizz	yes	web	jog	shut	chap	quiz	**this**	**too**	**they**
Date: Name:	chop	jazz	fox	wig	jet	shop	chat	**that**	**see**	**was**
Date: Name:	ship	chip	buzz	box	wag	jam	shin	**will**	**for**	**she**
Date: Name:	ring	sing	wing	king	bang	rang	long	**are**	**my**	**her**
Date: Name:	them	then	that	this	with	moth	thin	**you**	**they**	**all**

Phase 3(a) Supplementary Spelling List

N.B. Only to be used with children who are repeating aspects of this phase's work.

Source: Words 1 - 7 taken from Letters and Sounds Phase 3 Phonics
Words 8 - 10 taken from Letters and Sounds Phase 3 High Frequency Word List

	Week 1	Week 2	Week 3	Week 4	Week 5	Week 6
Date:						
Name:						
1	jam	van	fix	long	chin	buzz
2	jog	vet	mix	king	chip	fuzz
3	jet	zip	six	wing	much	fizz
4	jug	zap	box	sing	such	jazz
5	win	jam	fox	with	shop	quiz
6	web	Jill	yet	cloth	ship	quit
7	wag	Jack	yes	moth	shin	quick
8	**he**	**be**	**you**	**that**	**will**	**with**
9	**me**	**she**	**are**	**the**	**her**	**this**
10	**we**	**see**	**my**	**then**	**for**	**now**

Phase 3(a) Supplementary Spelling List

N.B. Only to be used with children who are repeating aspects of this phase's work.

Source: Words 1 - 7 taken from Letters and Sounds Phase 3 Phonics
Words 8 - 10 taken from Letters and Sounds Phase 3 High Frequency Word List

Date:
Name:

1. box
2. thin
3. chat
4. long
5. moth
6. yell
7. jazz
8. **all**
9. **are**
10. **my**

Date:
Name:

1. six
2. them
3. ring
4. fizz
5. win
6. such
7. zip
8. **was**
9. **you**
10. **they**

Date:
Name:

1. chap
2. king
3. yet
4. wax
5. wig
6. chin
7. jog
8. **for**
9. **see**
10. **look**

Date:
Name:

1. this
2. that
3. buzz
4. chat
5. fizz
6. yes
7. fox
8. **too**
9. **he**
10. **we**

Date:
Name:

1. then
2. that
3. shin
4. chop
5. jazz
6. chip
7. sing
8. **me**
9. **be**
10. **she**

Date:
Name:

1. jet
2. chin
3. quit
4. wag
5. mix
6. van
7. shut
8. **now**
9. **down**
10. **with**

Phase 3(b) Spelling List

Source: Words 1 - 7 taken from Letters and Sounds Phase 3 Phonics
Introducing: **ee, oo, ar, or, ai, oa.**
Words 8 - 10 taken from Letters and Sounds Phase 3 High Frequency Word List

	Week 1	Week 2	Week 3	Week 4	Week 5	Week 6
	Date:	Date:	Date:	Date:	Date:	Date:
	Name:	Name:	Name:	Name:	Name:	Name:
1	see	moon	car	or	rain	oak
2	feel	hoot	card	born	pain	coal
3	keep	boot	yard	for	hail	coat
4	sleep	cool	hard	fort	pail	goal
5	sheep	soon	farm	form	sail	soap
6	meet	spoon	arm	torn	fail	road
7	creep	school	harm	corn	wait	load
8	**was**	**all**	**see**	**me**	**too**	**for**
9	**she**	**they**	**my**	**we**	**look**	**down**
10	**be**	**you**	**are**	**he**	**her**	**now**

Phase 3(b) Spelling List

Source: Words 1 - 7 taken from Letters and Sounds Phase 3 Phonics
Introducing: **ur, oi, igh, ear, air, ure, er, ow.**
Words 8 - 10 taken from Letters and Sounds Phase 3 High Frequency Word List

Date:	Date:	Date:	Date:	Date:	Date:
Name:	Name:	Name:	Name:	Name:	Name:
1 fur	1 oil	1 high	1 now	1 ear	1 sure
2 burn	2 boil	2 sigh	2 how	2 dear	2 pure
3 hurt	3 coil	3 sight	3 cow	3 fear	3 cure
4 turn	4 soil	4 night	4 down	4 near	4 boxer
5 surf	5 toil	5 right	5 town	5 air	5 hammer
6 curl	6 coin	6 might	6 bow	6 fair	6 letter
7 urn	7 join	7 light	7 row	7 hair	7 dinner
8 **with**	8 **this**	8 **she**	8 **they**	8 **my**	8 **see**
9 **them**	9 **that**	9 **was**	9 **all**	9 **her**	9 **look**
10 **then**	10 **will**	10 **you**	10 **are**	10 **for**	10 **too**

Phase 3(b) Supplementary Spelling List

N.B. Only to be used with children who are repeating aspects of this phase's work.

Source: Words 1 - 7 taken from Letters and Sounds Phase 3 Phonics
Words 8 - 10 taken from Letters and Sounds Phase 3 High Frequency Word List

	Week 1	Week 2	Week 3	Week 4	Week 5	Week 6
	Date:	Date:	Date:	Date:	Date:	Date:
	Name:	Name:	Name:	Name:	Name:	Name:
1	see	or	burn	now	sure	card
2	keep	form	surf	town	pure	hard
3	meet	corn	curl	dear	her	for
4	moon	rain	boil	near	sister	born
5	car	coat	high	air	pool	fail
6	farm	soap	right	fair	soon	mail
7	harm	goat	light	hair	spoon	pain
8	**will**	**with**	**that**	**he**	**be**	**you**
9	**her**	**this**	**the**	**me**	**she**	**are**
10	**for**	**now**	**then**	**we**	**see**	**my**

Phase 3(b) Supplementary Spelling List

N.B. Only to be used with children who are repeating aspects of this phase's work.

Source: Words 1 - 7 taken from Letters and Sounds Phase 3 Phonics
Words 8 - 10 taken from Letters and Sounds Phase 3 High Frequency Word List

	Date: Name:	Date: Name:	Date: Name:	Date: Name:	Date: Name:	Date: Name:
1	now	boil	boot	boxer	curl	row
2	see	feel	cow	sleep	hammer	fair
3	car	hoot	yard	toil	meet	letter
4	or	card	sail	farm	spoon	school
5	oil	born	for	form	torn	hair
6	oak	how	load	fail	might	wait
7	fur	coal	fear	right	goat	join
8	**me**	**was**	**all**	**now**	**for**	**too**
9	**be**	**you**	**are**	**down**	**see**	**he**
10	**she**	**they**	**my**	**with**	**look**	**we**

‘Letters and Sounds’

Read and Spell High Frequency Words

Reinforcement Book 3a

Name: ______________

1 cat

2 bat

3 hat

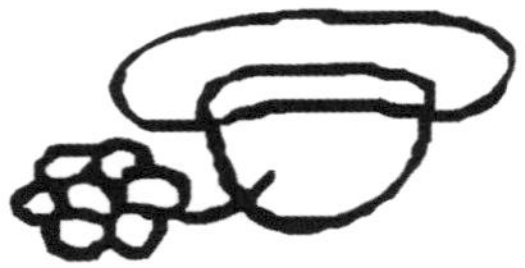

4 van

5 web

6 dog

7 pin

8 yak

9 jug

10 rug

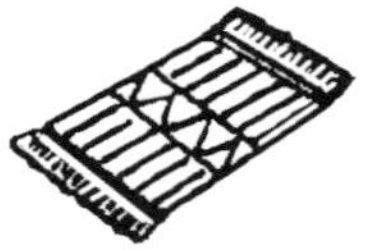

11 leg

12 sum

2 + 2 = 4

13 fox

14 quiz

?

'Letters and Sounds'

Read and Spell High Frequency Words

Reinforcement Book 3b

Name: ______________

1. will
2. that
3. this
4. then
5. them
6. with
7. now
8. down
9. for
10. see
11. look
12. too
13. he
14. we
15. me
16. be
17. she
18. was
19. you
20. they
21. all
22. are
23. my
24. her

Letters and Sounds Phase 3 Individual Pupil Record

Name: ______________________

Date Begun: ______________________

We can assume a letter or word has been learned when it has been either tested or used correctly at least 3 times.

Phase 3 Letter Progression	Tick or Date		
j			
v			
w			
x			
y			
z			
zz			
qu			

Phase 3 Consonant Digraphs	Tick or Date		
ch (chin)			
sh (shop)			
th (thin)			
th (this)			
ng (ring)			

Phase 3 Vowel Graphemes	Tick or Date		
ai (wait)			
ee (feel)			
igh (light)			
oa (coat)			
oo (food)			
oo (good)			
ar (bar)			
or (for)			
ur (burn)			
ow (down)			
oi (boil)			
ear (near)			
air (hair)			
ure (sure)			
-er (boxer)			

Phase 3 High Frequency Words	Tick or Date		
1. will			
2. that			
3. this			
4. then			
5. them			
6. with			
7. now			
8. down			
9. for			
10. see			
11. look			
12. too			
13. he			
14. we			
15. me			
16. be			
17. she			
18. was			
19. you			
20. they			
21. all			
22. are			
23. my			
24. her			

Bold indicates "Tricky" High Frequency Words

‘Letters and Sounds’

Phase 4

Phase 4 Spelling List

Source: Words 1 - 7 taken from Letters and Sounds Phase 4 Phonics
Introducing: **CVCC, CCVC, CCVCC, CCCVC AND CCCVCC words**
Words 8 - 10 taken from Letters and Sounds Phase 4 High Frequency Word List

	Week 1	Week 2	Week 3	Week 4	Week 5	Week 6
	Date: Name:	Date: Name:	Date: Name:	Date: Name:	Date: Name:	Date: Name:
1	tent	best	stop	coast	camp	green
2	bent	lost	step	roast	champ	steep
3	felt	cost	spin	toast	chimp	tree
4	belt	lift	spot	shrink	tramp	shoot
5	wind	gift	steep	blink	bench	school
6	band	soft	creep	think	punch	smooth
7	land	loft	sheep	thing	lunch	spoon
8	**went**	**help**	**come**	**so**	**said**	**little**
9	**from**	**children**	**where**	**do**	**have**	**one**
10	**just**	**it's**	**there**	**some**	**like**	**when**

Phase 4 Spelling List

Source: Words 1 - 7 taken from Letters and Sounds Phase 4 Phonics
Introducing: **CVCC, CCVC, CCVCC, CCCVC AND CCCVCC words**
Words 8 - 10 taken from Letters and Sounds Phase 4 High Frequency Word List

Date:	Date:	Date:	Date:	Date:	Date:
Name:	Name:	Name:	Name:	Name:	Name:
1 clown	1 smart	1 stand	1 munch	1 kept	1 helper
2 brown	2 star	2 brand	2 lunch	2 crept	2 steeper
3 frown	3 dart	3 blend	3 crunch	3 slept	3 shorter
4 crown	4 park	4 spend	4 strap	4 thank	4 stronger
5 growl	5 shark	5 trust	5 spring	5 blank	5 shelter
6 crash	6 sport	6 crust	6 string	6 blink	6 softer
7 flash	7 short	7 fluster	7 strong	7 think	7 smarter
8 **out**	8 **like**	8 **it's**	8 **just**	8 **do**	8 **one**
9 **what**	9 **have**	9 **children**	9 **from**	9 **come**	9 **some**
10 **so**	10 **said**	10 **help**	10 **went**	10 **there**	10 **where**

Phase 4 Spelling Supplementary List

N.B. Only to be used with children who are repeating aspects of this phase's work.

Source: Words 1 - 7 taken from Letters and Sounds Phase 4 Phonic
Revising: **CVCC, CCVC, CCVCC, CCCVC AND CCCVCC words**
Words 8 - 10 taken from Letters and Sounds Phase 4 High Frequency Word List

	Week 1	Week 2	Week 3	Week 4	Week 5	Week 6
	Date:	Date:	Date:	Date:	Date:	Date:
	Name:	Name:	Name:	Name:	Name:	Name:
1	flash	short	fluster	strap	spend	park
2	land	loft	lunch	spoon	sheep	thing
3	brand	tent	best	stop	coast	camp
4	brown	star	branch	steeper	crept	lunch
5	fluster	strong	think	crust	sport	much
6	strap	thank	stronger	slip	spring	crash
7	spring	blank	shelter	clip	step	roast
8	**children**	**from**	**so**	**like**	**little**	**come**
9	**help**	**went**	**do**	**have**	**one**	**were**
10	**what**	**just**	**some**	**out**	**when**	**there**

‘Letters and Sounds’

Read and Spell High Frequency Words

Reinforcement Book 4

Name: ____________

1 went

2 from

3 just

4 help

5 children

6 it’s

7 said

8 have

9 like

10 so

11 do

12 some

13 come

14 were

15 there

16 little

17 one

18 when

19 out

20 what

Letters and Sounds Phase 4 Individual Pupil Record

We can assume a letter or word has been learned when it has been either tested or used correctly at least 3 times.

Name: ______________________

Date Begun: ______________________

Phase 4 CVCC words	Tick or Date		
-ng (ring)			
-ld (bold)			
-nd (land)			
-lk (milk)			
-nk (think)			
-sk (flask)			
-lp (help)			
-mp (jump)			
-sp (lisp)			
-ct (fact)			
-ft (lift)			
-lt (belt)			
-nt (bent)			
-pt (kept)			
-st (lost)			
-xt (next)			
-lf (self)			
-nch (bunch)			
-lth (health)			

Phase 4 CCVC words	Tick or Date		
bl- (black)			
br- (brick)			
cl (clap)			
cr- (crab)			
dr- (drop)			
dw- (dwell)			
fl- (flag)			
fr- (frog)			
gl- (glad)			
gr- (grin)			
pl- (plum)			
pr- (pram)			
sc- (scab)			
sk- (skip)			
sl- (slip)			
sm- (smack)			
sn- (snap)			
sp- (spot)			
st- (stop)			
sw- (swim)			
tr- (trip)			
tw- (twin)			

Phase 4 CCCVC & CCCVCC words	Tick or Date		
scr- (scrap)			
shr- (shred)			
spl- (splash)			
spr- (spring)			
squ- (squash)			
str- (string)			
thr- (thrush)			

Phase 4 High Frequency Words	Tick or Date		
1. went			
2. from			
3. just			
4. help			
5. children			
6. it's			
7. said			
8. have			
9. like			
10. so			
11. do			
12. some			
13. come			
14. were			
15. there			
16. little			
17. one			
18. when			
19. out			
20. what			

Bold indicates "Tricky" High Frequency Words

'Letters and Sounds'

Phase 5

Phase 5 Spelling List 1

Source: Words 1 - 10 taken from Letters and Sounds Phase 5 Phonics Introducing alternative spellings for phonemes.
Words 11 - 12 taken from Letters and Sounds Phase 5 High Frequency Word List

	Week 1	Week 2	Week 3	Week 4	Week 5	Week 6
	Date:	Date:	Date:	Date:	Date:	Date:
	Name:	Name:	Name:	Name:	Name:	Name:
1	play	pie	boy	blue	when	blew
2	day	lie	toy	clue	what	chew
3	clay	tie	joy	glue	which	grew
4	stray	die	enjoy	true	why	drew
5	spray	cried	annoy	value	where	knew
6	out	sea	girl	law	who	flew
7	about	seat	sir	jaw	wheel	threw
8	cloud	bead	bird	paw	toe	elephant
9	found	read	skirt	lawn	doe	dolphin
10	sound	treat	first	yawn	goes	alphabet
11	**old**	**I'm**	**house**	**made**	**time**	**your**
12	**don't**	**by**	**about**	**make**	**came**	**day**

Phase 5 Spelling List 1

Source: Words 1 - 10 taken from Letters and Sounds Phase 5 Phonics
Introducing alternative spellings for phonemes.
Words 11 - 12 taken from Letters and Sounds Phase 5 High Frequency Word List

Date:	Date:	Date:	Date:	Date:	Date:
Name:	Name:	Name:	Name:	Name:	Name:
1 key	1 take	1 bone	1 fast	1 he	1 full
2 keys	2 game	2 pole	2 grass	2 she	2 bull
3 monkey	3 same	3 home	3 path	3 me	3 pull
4 donkey	4 name	4 alone	4 bath	4 mind	4 bush
5 money	5 snake	5 those	5 bacon	5 find	5 push
6 honey	6 even	6 use	6 lady	6 wild	6 unit
7 chimney	7 these	7 rule	7 wash	7 old	7 music
8 Paul	8 ripe	8 June	8 want	8 cold	8 stupid
9 August	9 pipe	9 cube	9 watch	9 gold	9 tuba
10 haunt	10 pine	10 tube	10 wasp	10 fold	10 duty
11 **here**	11 **saw**	11 **oh**	11 **Mr.**	11 **cooked**	11 **asked**
12 **very**	12 **put**	12 **their**	12 **Mrs.**	12 **called**	12 **could**

Phase 5 Spelling List 2

Source: Words 1 - 10 taken from Letters and Sounds Phase 5 Phonics Introducing alternative spellings for phonemes.
Words 11 - 12 taken from Letters and Sounds Phases 3-5 High Frequency Word List

	Week 1	Week 2	Week 3	Week 4	Week 5	Week 6
	Date:	Date:	Date:	Date:	Date:	Date:
	Name:	Name:	Name:	Name:	Name:	Name:
1	low	head	could	very	school	catch
2	grow	dead	would	happy	Christmas	patch
3	snow	bread	should	smelly	chemist	pitch
4	show	ready	soup	lolly	nice	witch
5	slow	instead	group	merry	mice	stitch
6	chief	her	by	cherry	price	nature
7	brief	fern	my	ferry	gem	future
8	thief	herb	try	carry	gent	picture
9	field	verb	dry	gym	magic	mixture
10	shield	kerb	fry	crystal	danger	adventure
11	**will**	**that**	**this**	**then**	**them**	**with**
12	**went**	**from**	**just**	**help**	**children**	**it's**

Phase 5 Spelling List 2

Source: Words 1 - 10 taken from Letters and Sounds Phase 5 Phonics
Introducing alternative spellings for phonemes.
Words 11 - 12 taken from Letters and Sounds Phases 3-5 High Frequency Word List

Date:	Date:	Date:	Date:	Date:	Date:
Name:	Name:	Name:	Name:	Name:	Name:
1 *fudge*	1 knit	1 wrap	1 listen	1 some	1 beer
2 nudge	2 knot	2 wrong	2 whistle	2 come	2 deer
3 badge	3 knee	3 write	3 bristle	3 done	3 cheer
4 bridge	4 knife	4 wrote	4 rustle	4 month	4 *father*
5 hedge	5 know	5 wreck	5 bustle	5 Monday	5 rather
6 lamb	6 knew	6 house	6 castle	6 mother	6 all
7 comb	7 knight	7 mouse	7 happy	7 brother	7 ball
8 climb	8 gnat	8 horse	8 sunny	8 ease	8 *fall*
9 crumb	9 gnash	9 nurse	9 mummy	9 tease	9 call
10 thumb	10 sign	10 purse	10 daddy	10 please	10 hall
11 **now**	11 **down**	11 **your**	11 ***for***	11 **time**	11 **so**
12 **said**	12 **have**	12 **old**	12 **like**	12 **see**	12 **come**

Phase 5 Spelling List 3

Source: Words 1 - 10 taken from Letters and Sounds Phase 5 Phonics
Introducing alternative spellings for phonemes.
Words 11 - 12 taken from Letters and Sounds Phases 3- 5 High Frequency Word List

	Week 1	Week 2	Week 3	Week 4	Week 5	Week 6
Date:						
Name:						
1	half	pear	four	caught	learn	sure
2	calm	bear	pour	taught	earn	sugar
3	palm	wear	your	naughty	earth	passion
4	bare	tear	court	daughter	heard	session
5	care	always	there	word	search	mission
6	fare	also	where	work	mention	usual
7	scare	almost	nowhere	world	station	casual
8	share	talk	somewhere	worm	position	visual
9	hare	walk	everywhere	worth	special	vision
10	square	chalk	anywhere	worst	social	television
11	**look**	**came**	**I'm**	**were**	**little**	**she**
12	**do**	**some**	**we**	**house**	**saw**	**one**

Phase 5 Supplementary Spelling List

N.B. Only to be used with children who are repeating aspects of this phase's work.

Source: Words 1 - 10 taken from Letters and Sounds Phase 5 Phonics Introducing alternative spellings for phonemes.
Words 11 - 12 taken from Letters and Sounds High Frequency Word List

Date:	Date:	Date:	Date:	Date:	Date:
Name:	Name:	Name:	Name:	Name:	Name:
1 nice	1 same	1 for	1 bar	1 book	1 feel
2 mice	2 name	2 fort	2 car	2 took	2 heel
3 slice	3 shame	3 forty	3 card	3 wood	3 week
4 price	4 tame	4 born	4 hard	4 boot	4 need
5 hide	5 bake	5 corn	5 garden	5 shoot	5 steep
6 ride	6 cake	6 torn	6 arm	6 broom	6 sweep
7 mile	7 make	7 more	7 farm	7 bedroom	7 street
8 smile	8 face	8 story	8 harm	8 roof	8 screen
9 drive	9 shake	9 morning	9 alarm	9 pool	9 speed
10 driver	10 snake	10 forgot	10 smart	10 stool	10 queen
11 **pulled**	11 **fell**	11 **well**	11 **long**	11 **next**	11 **duck**
12 **miss**	12 **still**	12 **tell**	12 **along**	12 **lots**	12 **best**

Phase 5 Supplementary Spelling List

N.B. Only to be used with children who are repeating aspects of this phase's work.

Source: Words 1 - 10 taken from Letters and Sounds Phase 5 Phonics Introducing alternative spellings for phonemes.
Words 11 - 12 taken from Letters and Sounds High Frequency Word List

	Week 1	Week 2	Week 3	Week 4	Week 5	Week 6
	Date:	Date:	Date:	Date:	Date:	Date:
	Name:	Name:	Name:	Name:	Name:	Name:
1	cone	tube	due	rain	oats	dirty
2	tone	cube	cue	pain	coat	third
3	phone	tune	hue	again	goal	first
4	stone	flute	blue	paint	coal	girl
5	note	huge	glue	chain	foal	dirt
6	rose	rule	clue	nail	road	shirt
7	nose	rude	true	sail	roast	thirty
8	close	cute	value	tail	toast	thirteen
9	rope	tunes	statue	afraid	soak	skirt
10	hope	June	argue	explain	soaking	thirsty
11	**fish**	**must**	**think**	**stop**	**last**	**wind**
12	**wish**	**much**	**thing**	**gran**	**fast**	**king**

Phase 5 Supplementary Spelling List

N.B. Only to be used with children who are repeating aspects of this phase's work.

Source: Words 1 - 10 taken from Letters and Sounds Phase 5 Phonics List Introducing alternative spellings for phonemes.
Words 11 - 12 taken from Letters and Sounds High Frequency Word List

Date:
Name:

1 toil
2 foil
3 boil
4 coil
5 soil
6 spoil
7 noise
8 choice
9 voice
10 toilet
11 **dragon**
12 **grandad**

Date:
Name:

1 jaw
2 law
3 paw
4 saw
5 dawn
6 dawning
7 straw
8 awful
9 crawl
10 yawn
11 **plants**
12 **eggs**

Date:
Name:

1 say
2 day
3 way
4 clay
5 away
6 today
7 stray
8 crayon
9 delay
10 spray
11 **play**
12 **may**

Date:
Name:

1 fur
2 curl
3 burn
4 burnt
5 church
6 nurse
7 purse
8 turn
9 turning
10 turned
11 **things**
12 **something**

Date:
Name:

1 tea
2 sea
3 teach
4 reach
5 cream
6 scream
7 clean
8 mean
9 please
10 pleased
11 **across**
12 **away**

Date:
Name:

1 out
2 shout
3 about
4 house
5 mouse
6 mouth
7 south
8 sound
9 around
10 aloud
11 **say**
12 **way**

‘Letters and Sounds’

Read and Spell High Frequency Words

Reinforcement Book 5

Name: ____________

1 old

2 don’t

3 I’m

4 by

5 time

6 house

7 about

8 your

9 day

10 made

11 came

12 make

13 here

14 saw

15 very

16 put

17 oh

18 their

19 people

20 Mr.

21 Mrs.

22 looked

23 called

24 asked

25 could

Letters and Sounds Phase 5 Individual Pupil Record

Name: ______________________

Date Begun: ______________________

We can assume a letter or word has been learned when it has been either tested or used correctly at least 3 times.

Phase 5 - Graphemes and Phonemes - alternative spellings

	Tick or Date		
Vowel Graphemes			
ay (day)			
ou (out)			
ie (pie)			
ea (sea)			
ir (girl)			
ue (clue)			
ue (cue)			
aw (saw)			
wh (when)			
wh (who)			
ph (photo)			
ew (blew)			
oe (toe)			
au (author)			
ey (money)			
a-e (came)			
e-e (these)			
-e (like)			
-e (bone)			
-e (tube)			
(acorn)			
(he)			
(mind)			
(gold)			
(unit)			
(was)			
** (fast)			
** (put)			
w (down)			
(chief)			
a (head)			
r (herb)			
u (you)			
u (could)			
u (mould)			
(by)			
(gym)			
(happy)			
(school)			
(chef)			
(cell)			
(gent)			
(grey)			

	Tick or Date		
Alternative Spellings for each Phoneme			
/ch/ (picture)			
/ch/ (catch)			
/j/ (fudge)			
/m/ lamb			
/n/ gnat			
/n/ knit			
/r/ wrap			
/s/ listen			
/s/ house			
/z/ please			
/u/** some			
/i/ happy			
/i/ donkey			
/ear/ here			
/ear/ beer			
/ar/ father			
/ar/ half			
/air/ there			
/air/ pear			
/air/ bare			
/or/ all			
/or/ four			
/or/ caught			
/ur/ learn			
/ur/ word			
/oo/ could			
/oo/ put			
/ai/ day			
/ai/ came			
/ea/ sea			
/ea/ these			
/ea/ happy			
/ea/ chief			
/ea/ key			
/igh/ pie			
/igh/ by			
/igh/ like			
/oa/ low			
/oa/ toe			

	Tick or Date		
/oa/ bone			
/(y)oo/ cue			
/(y)oo/ tune			
/(y)oo/ stew			
/oo/ clue			
/oo/ June			
/oo/ blew			
/sh/ special			
/sh/ station			
/sh/ sure			
/sh/ passion			
/sh/ chef			
Phase 5 High Frequency Words			
1. old			
2. don't			
3. I'm			
4. by			
5. time			
6. house			
7. about			
8. your			
9. day			
10. made			
11. came			
12. make			
13. here			
14. saw			
15. very			
16. put (south)			
17. oh			
18. their			
19. people			
20. Mr.			
21. Mrs.			
22. looked			
23. called			
24. asked			
25. could			

Bold indicates "Tricky" High Frequency Words ***South of England only*

‘Letters and Sounds’

Phase 6

Phase 6 Spelling List 1

Source: Words 1 - 10 taken from Letters and Sounds Phase 6 Phonics - suffixes
Words 11 - 12 taken from Letters and Sounds Phase 5 High Frequency Word List

	Week 1	Week 2	Week 3	Week 4	Week 5	Week 6
	Date:	Date:	Date:	Date:	Date:	Date:
	Name:	Name:	Name:	Name:	Name:	Name:
1	stop	stops	fizz	fizzes	bake	baked
2	stops	parks	fizzes	whizzes	baked	waved
3	park	chats	cross	buzzes	wave	hoped
4	parks	sings	crosses	crosses	waved	smiled
5	bunch	wings	cry	flosses	hope	tiled
6	bunches	bunches	cries	misses	hoped	filed
7	crash	lunches	cried	kisses	smile	faced
8	crashes	crunches	try	tries	smiled	raced
9	match	catches	tries	dries	save	saved
10	matches	matches	tried	fries	saved	shaved
11	**old**	**I'm**	**time**	**your**	**made**	**looked**
12	**don't**	**by**	**house**	**day**	**make**	**called**

(N.B: Some plurals repeated

Phase 6 Spelling List 1

Source: Words 1 - 10 taken from Letters and Sounds Phase 6 Phonics - suffixes
Words 11 - 12 taken from Letters and Sounds Phase 5 High Frequency Word List

Name:	Date: Name:	Date: Name:	Date: Name:	Date: Name:	Date: Name:
1 like	1 liking	1 put	1 putting	1 play	1 playing
2 liking	2 hiking	2 putting	2 shutting	2 playing	2 staying
3 hope	3 hoping	3 clap	3 clapping	3 blow	3 blowing
4 hoping	4 coping	4 clapping	4 flapping	4 blowing	4 knowing
5 come	5 coming	5 slim	5 slimming	5 heat	5 heating
6 coming	6 baking	6 slimming	6 swimming	6 heating	6 beating
7 bake	7 making	7 stop	7 stopping	7 sail	7 sailing
8 baking	8 taking	8 stopping	8 shopping	8 sailing	8 emailing
9 wave	9 waving	9 get	9 getting	9 moan	9 moaning
10 waving	10 shaving	10 getting	10 letting	10 moaning	10 groaning
11 **your**	11 **made**	11 **looked**	11 **old**	11 **I'm**	11 **time**
12 **day**	12 **make**	12 **called**	12 **don't**	12 **by**	12 **house**
	(N.B: Some plurals repeated without the root word.)		*(N.B: Some plurals repeated without the root word.)*		*(N.B: Some plurals repeated without the root word.)*

Phase 6 Spelling List 2

Source: Words 1 - 10 taken from Letters and Sounds Phase 6 Phonics - suffixes
Words 11 - 12 taken from Letters and Sounds Phase 5 High Frequency Word List

	Week 1	Week 2	Week 3	Week 4	Week 5	Week 6
Date:						
Name:						
1	worry	worried	flap	flapped	sing	singing
2	worried	hurried	flapped	hopped	singing	kicking
3	hurry	carried	hop	skipped	kick	jumping
4	hurried	married	hopped	ripped	kicking	starting
5	carry	copied	skip	bumped	start	lifting
6	carried	buried	skipped	batted	starting	shifting
7	marry	ferried	rip	spotted	lift	laughing
8	married	cried	ripped	fitted	lifting	fighting
9	copy	tried	jump	jumped	fight	flying
10	copied	dried	jumped	started	fighting	spying
11	**called**	**made**	**very**	**here**	**could**	**asked**
12	**oh**	**by**	**people**	**day**	**I'm**	**saw**

(N.B. Some plurals repeated

Phase 6 Spelling List 2

Source: Words 1 - 10 taken from Letters and Sounds Phase 6 Phonics - suffixes
Words 11 - 12 taken from Letters and Sounds Phase 5 High Frequency Word List

Date:
Name:

1	fun
2	funny
3	sun
4	sunny
5	number
6	runner
7	bigger
8	waiter
9	later
10	writer
11	**very**
12	**people**

Date:
Name:

1	knife
2	knives
3	elf
4	elves
5	shelf
6	shelves
7	half
8	halves
9	calf
10	calves
11	**made**
12	**by**

Date:
Name:

1	smoke
2	smoky
3	nose
4	nosy
5	shake
6	shaky
7	taste
8	tasty
9	ice
10	icy
11	**called**
12	**oh**

Date:
Name:

1	darkness
2	blackness
3	kindness
4	sadness
5	madness
6	silliness
7	happiness
8	payment
9	argument
10	statement
11	**asked**
12	**saw**

Date:
Name:

1	deadly
2	safely
3	wisely
4	happily
5	sleepily
6	wishful
7	mindful
8	dreadful
9	handful
10	skilful
11	**could**
12	**I'm**

Name:

1	careful
2	carefully
3	hopeful
4	hopefully
5	playful
6	playfully
7	fearful
8	fearfully
9	joyful
10	joyfully
11	**here**
12	**day**

Phase 6 Supplementary Spelling List

N.B. Only to be used with children who are repeating aspects of this phase's work.
Source: Words 1 - 10 taken from Letters and Sounds Phase 6 Phonics - suffixes
Words 11 - 12 taken from Letters and Sounds High Frequency Word List

	Week 1	Week 2	Week 3	Week 4	Week 5	Week 6
Date:						
Name:						
1	bad	badly	lazy	lazier	hope	careful
2	badly	deadly	lazier	crazier	hopeful	hopeful
3	dead	deeply	laziest	heavier	care	wasteful
4	deadly	safely	heavy	cloudier	careful	playful
5	deep	wisely	heavier	messier	play	harmful
6	deeply	happily	heaviest	laziest	playful	fearful
7	safe	funnily	messy	craziest	pity	faithful
8	safely	sleepily	messier	heaviest	pitiful	plentiful
9	wise	crazily	messiest	cloudiest	plenty	pitiful
10	wisely	lazily	messily	messiest	plentiful	beautiful
11	**along**	**king**	**gran**	**much**	**dragon**	**well**
12	**must**	**fast**	**wish**	**things**	**something**	**think**

(N.B. Some plurals repeated

Phase 6 Supplementary Spelling List

N.B. Only to be used with children who are repeating aspects of this phase's work.

Source: Words 1 - 10 taken from Letters and Sounds Phase 6 Phonics - suffixes
Words 11 - 12 taken from Letters and Sounds High Frequency Word List

	1	2	3	4	5	6	7	8	9	10	11	12
Date: Name:	number	runner	bigger	darkness	blackness	sadness	kindness	payment	pavement	statement	**pulled**	**next**
Date: Name:	careful	playful	hopeful	carefully	playfully	hopefully	deadly	safely	happily	sleepily	**lots**	**still**
Date: Name:	singing	kicking	licking	hoping	making	putting	swimming	shopping	stopping	clapping	**fell**	**stop**
Date: Name:	baked	waved	saved	behaved	whipped	jumped	camped	started	hurried	worried	**last**	**fish**
Date: Name:	knives	wives	elves	shelves	calves	halves	smoky	nosy	shaky	tasty	**best**	**long**
Name:	parks	stops	fizzes	buzzes	foxes	kisses	crosses	munches	lunches	matches	**duck**	**miss**

'Letters and Sounds'

Read and Spell High Frequency Words

Reinforcement Book 6

Name: ____________

1. ran
2. man
3. bad
4. hat
5. sat
6. cat
7. has
8. did
9. bed
10. red
11. yes
12. let
13. dog
14. top
15. hot
16. boy
17. fox
18. box
19. fun
20. sun
21. run
22. am
23. us
24. end
25. it's
26. well
27. tell
28. fell
29. still
30. pulled
31. miss
32. duck
33. best
34. next

'Letters and Sounds' Read and Spell High Frequency Words

Reinforcement Book 7

Name: ____________

1. lots
2. stop
3. long
4. along
5. last
6. fast
7. gran
8. wind
9. king
10. must
11. fish
12. wish
13. much
14. thing
15. things
16. think
17. something
18. plants
19. eggs
20. dragon
21. grandad
22. rabbit
23. across
24. say
25. way
26. away
27. play
28. may
29. gave
30. take
31. baby
32. again
33. or
34. before

‘Letters and Sounds’
Read and Spell High Frequency Words

Reinforcement Book 8

Name: ______________

1. more
2. morning
3. only
4. over
5. cold
6. told
7. most
8. home
9. going
10. grow
11. window
12. coat
13. find
14. inside
15. white
16. liked
17. night
18. right
19. car
20. park
21. hard
22. live
23. lived
24. gone
25. after
26. never
27. under
28. better
29. river
30. other
31. another
32. mother
33. tree
34. trees

'Letters and Sounds' Read and Spell High Frequency Words

Reinforcement Book 9

Name: ____________

1 there
2 need
3 been
4 sleep
5 keep

6 sheep
7 feet
8 green
9 tea
10 sea

11 eat
12 each
13 really
14 please
15 great

16 bear
17 head
18 soon
19 room
20 food

21 school
22 book
23 took
24 look
25 looking

26 door
27 good
28 found
29 round
30 around

31 our
32 mouse
33 shouted
34 town

'Letters and Sounds'

Read and Spell High Frequency Wordss

Reinforcement Book 10

Name: ____________

1 how
2 snow
3 know
4 would
5 couldn't

6 let's
7 I'll
8 didn't
9 we're
10 I've

11 can't
12 that's
13 there's
14 he's
15 girl

16 first
17 birds
18 who
19 why
20 which

21 where
22 want
23 wanted
24 ever

25 every
26 everyone
27 any
28 many

29 once
30 place
31 magic
32 giant

‘Letters and Sounds’
Read and Spell High Frequency Words

Reinforcement Book 11

Name: ______________

1. even
2. began
3. than
4. these
5. jumped
6. stopped
7. laughed
8. cried
9. thought
10. through
11. key
12. small
13. because
14. water
15. air
16. suddenly
17. work
18. new
19. two
20. fl[illegible]
21. use
22. different
23. coming
24. floppy
25. garden
26. animals
27. friends
28. horse
29. narrator
30. clothes
31. eyes
32. dark

Letters and Sounds Individual Pupil Record

We can assume a letter or word has been learned when it has been either tested or used correctly at least 3 times.

Name: ______________________

Date Begun: ______________________

Phase 6
Adding Suffixes (remember there are always exceptions)

Plurals			**Tick or Date**		
stop	stops	add s			
fizz, box	fizzes, boxes	add es			
hurry	hurries	change y to i and add es			
knife	knives	change f to v and add s			
-ed words					
mess	messed	words ending in two consonants just add ed			
show, play	showed, played	words ending in a long vowel sound just add ed			
bake	baked	words ending in e just add d			
worry	worried	words ending in y (unless a long vowel sound) change y to i and add ed			
hop, plot	hopped	words ending in a consonant with a short vowel sound, double the consonant and add ed			
-ing words					
sing	singing	words ending in two consonants just add ing			
blow	blowing	words ending in a long vowel sound just add ing			
like	liking	words ending in e - drop e and add ing			
put	putting	words ending in a consonant with a short vowel sound, double the consonant and add ing			
-y words (N.B. -y acts like a vowel)					
sand	sandy	words ending in two consonants just add y			
snow	snowy	words ending in a long vowel sound just add y			
smoke	smoky	words ending in e -drop e add y			
fun	funny	words ending in a consonant with a short vowel sound, double the consonant and add y			
-er words					
post	poster	words ending in two consonants just add er			
slow, play	slower, player	words with long vowel sound just add er			
write	writer	words ending in e just add r			
happy	happier	words ending in y (unless a long vowel sound) change y to i and add er			
run	runner	words ending in a consonant with a short vowel sound, double the consonant and add er			
-est words					
strict	strictest	words ending in two consonants just add est			
slow	slowest	words ending in a long vowel sound just add est			
late	latest	words ending in e just add st			
happy	happiest	words ending in y (unless a long vowel sound) change y to i and add est			
big	biggest	words ending in a consonant with a short vowel sound, double the consonant and add est			
-ly words					
sad	sadly	just add ly			
careful	carefully	just add ly			
safe	safely	keep the e and add ly			
happy	happily	words endind in y - change y to i and add ly			
-ment					
pay	payment	just add ment			
amuse	amusement	keep the e and add ment			
-ness					
dark	darkness	just add ness			
happy	happiness	words ending in y - change y to i and add ness			
-ful (at the end of a word - remember, only one 'l')					
rest	restful	just add ful			
care	careful	keep the e and add ful			
play	playful	words ending in a long vowel sound just add ful			
beauty	beautiful	words ending in y (unless a long vowel sound) change y to i and add ful			